Bipolar Express

Mulpurinni Doris Kartinyeri

Bipolar Express
From One Mind to Another

Acknowledgements

I thank Sue Anderson and Mike Lawson and Ginninderra Press for their help and support in bringing this book to publication.

Bipolar Express: From One Mind to Another
ISBN 978 1 76041 343 9
Copyright © Mulpurinni Doris Kartinyeri 2017

First published 2017 by
GINNINDERRA PRESS
PO Box 3461 Port Adelaide 5015
www.ginninderrapress.com.au

Contents

Writing this book	9
My background	11
My journey begins	12
Did I hear right?	13
An early episode	14
Aboriginal women and connections	17
Straw hat	19
Strength and energy	20
The gift of bipolar	21
My child	22
The illness is like this	23
My children and my illness	24
Family relationships	26
Effect on the family	27
Family	28
Manic episodes	29
More manic attacks	31
Mood swings	32
An early mood swing	34
Manic behaviour	36
Bipolar writing	37
Manic attacks	38
Dark and light	39
Manic again	40
Thinking back	41
This is me	42
Being stolen	43

The seasons	45
Medication	46
The situation of bipolar patients	49
More history	51
Camp Coorong	53
Understanding the illness: 2008	54
Depression	56
Me and my leaders	57
Shades of colour	59
Looking for help	60
Colebrook	61
Doreen	62
John	63
In hospital	64
Writing	66
I don't know that person	69
The battles of mental illness	70
Mental health	71
Money and mind	72
The younger generation	73
The seasons	74
Managing my illness	75
The colour of laughter	76
A journey of healing	77
Dispossession	78
My culture	79
Friends help the healing	80
Being drug-free	81
I lost my culture, the white fella way	82
More highs and the lows	83
It's just the beginning	86
Depression	87
After the manic episode	89

On the way up again	90
Being active in the community	92
Looking at myself	94
Friends with mental illness	96
The need for help	98
Shame	99
Friends	100
Sharing with my people	101
Walk with respect	102
Kumerangk	103
Hospitalisation	104
Hospital again	106
Trauma	108
Decisions	109
The day begins	110
The future	111

Dedication

Writing this book has been a huge task for me, to bring everything together on this difficult topic. I have had input from friends and my family, who have many, many times witnessed my antics when on my so-called 'trips' and journeys. I must acknowledge all the support I have received from my immediate families, from Jennadene, John and Tanya. As a grieving mother and grandmother, for many years I travelled a painful journey to connect with my family. In my family there were seven children. I was the youngest, with two older sisters, Connie and Doreen, both deceased. My youngest daughter Tanya (now deceased) blossomed into a beautiful young mother who worked hard at connecting to her babies, Jade, Paige and Bella. This book is for them and the families of Jennadene and John. There are sixteen grandchildren and great-grandchildren, with one deceased, Rhys. I dedicate this book to my family and my grandchildren and great-grandchildren. I am sure I have tried them all with endless phone calls and my endless visits to doctors and hospitals. When I become unwell, I suffer tremendously but my children and my family suffer too. I have also been supported by many of my friends during my late-night romps, which they have had to cope with and be sympathetic towards me. I have also had support from those who have had personal experiences themselves with mental illness.

Writing this book

I was awake with excitement in 2002 when I received a grant for writing. I was officially recognised as a fifty-seven-year-old Indigenous author. The writing would help me try to understand my illness.

I write with the best of my ability and try to validate the true essence of myself and of this illness as an Indigenous woman. I am enthusiastic about telling my story all about my illness – bipolar mood swing disorder. I write with restlessness and with recklessness, sometimes with energy so strong, along with energy incredibly low. With the effect of this illness comes the need to rebuild myself and my self-esteem, and finally to come to terms with the illness itself.

I get angry and so frustrated at times. I want people with mental illness to be acknowledged and treated with respect, understanding and compassion. We are strong people who deserve to be trusted. And I want for those who are not coping and who need constant reassurance throughout their illnesses to be able to feel worthy. I write this book for all bipolar sufferers and for all those who suffer anxiety and for those who are pessimistic towards every issue surrounding mental health.

I now reach out as a writer, an author, a poet and as a mother and a proud grandmother of eighteen, and great-grandmother of one. This is my story, my personal experience of coping with isolation, in my state of mind; no one could or would bother to ask me how I felt. I am going to tell it my way so that you can read and understand about mental illness at grass roots level.

I want to tell the world of my journey of misfortune, of the years of pain and sorrow and of my attempts to manage an illness that can affect me at any time. I try to live a fruitful and productive life following the motto of the three Ls – Look, Listen and Learn. This is the third book

I have written. The first, *Kick the Tin*, was an autobiography of my early life. The second was an illustrated children's book called *Bush Games and Knuckle Bones*. I am proud to say that I was invited as guest speaker for 2004 at the Writers Week festival in Adelaide. This is a great honour for me, a recognition of myself as a Ngarrindjeri writer. I stood and was proud.

I write to share my experiences as an ordinary, normal, everyday person and also as an extraordinary woman when I am consumed with this illness. This is a huge challenge for me. I want to take you the reader through a journey into a world of really confronting issues experienced by someone suffering with bipolar. To all those who have grieved and who have suffered mental anguish from the loss of family, this is for you. My direction in life has been on such a journey of connecting with my soul, and focusing on my needs and my well-being. I write about my own experiences and what I have learned. I try to comprehend as much as I can. These are my writings as who I am.

My background

I am an Aboriginal woman born in September 1945, a member of the Stolen Generations in Australia. I am a proud indigenous Ngarrindjeri woman, proud to tell my story.

Both my parents were from Point McLeay, known as Raukkan. My father was Oswald Kartinyeri and my mother Thelma Kartinyeri, née Rigney. My sisters were Nancy, Doreen and Connie and my brothers Oscar and Ronald. In my family there were six children. I was the youngest. I am privileged and honoured in accepting a beautiful name, such a beautiful spiritual name. Dr Doreen Kartinyeri, my older sister, gave me a skin name passed down from my great, great grandmother, Mulpurinni, a name that I am honoured to have and use.

At the age of a few months, I was removed from my family and raised in a government home for removed Aboriginal children, at Colebrook Home in Eden Hills, a suburb of Adelaide. I was there until I was sixteen. Then I was released into the big wide world, displaced and alone. I feel myself that the crucial fibre of my existence was not woven into the fabric of my people and family. I was innocent and naïve. Maybe this was when the seed of my illness was planted.

I have had this illness for nearly thirty years and have tried with trials and errors to accept it and to come to terms with this at times frightening illness. With no knowledge and understanding I try to come to terms with this illness that can be so dreadful and bizarre. I have endured many years of appointments with doctors and psychiatrists, late-night hospital ward admissions and spells in mental hospitals. It is a disease which has caused destruction and disruptions throughout my life and in my family. Believe me, it can be frightening. At first it happened in isolated bouts, I received no warning and had to educate myself about it.

My journey begins

I need to help you begin your journey with me. So I will start by explaining the concept of this book in relation to my imagination. I am an Indigenous woman connected to my land spiritually and I have a spiritual connection to the polar bear for some unknown reason. To me the polar bear has a pure essence and my creativity is stimulated by this thought. My Indigenous spirit, me and the polar bear combine to represent who I am. The concept of the wonderful title of this book that emerged at the time of my initial diagnosis reflects the way I think with my mood swings.

Did I hear right?

I entered the doctor's surgery. I had become unwell and snowed under once again at my daughter's place in Murray Bridge, apparently picking weeds like they were flowers and walking around in circles chanting. My movements, my thoughts, are dormant as I enter the surgery. I was aware of my surroundings as I sat motionless with my eldest daughter Jennadene while we sat quietly together in the waiting room.

'The doctor's ready, Mum,' she said softly to me.

Very little was said between us. I just sat waiting like a child. My daughter and the doctor were discussing my illness. I overheard them as I walked towards the exit door to leave. I turned quickly to respond to what was being said between my daughter and the doctor,

On hearing the word bipolar, and speaking out loud and clear with a loud chuckle, I said, 'What, all the way from Poland!' and I gave the doctor a bear hug of reassurance.

I saw the funny side as the session with the doctor came to an end. I knew I was unwell. This was real to me. I really did think this illness actally came from Poland.

It is difficult to timeline my illness, as in some parts of the year I am functioning well and in the other parts I am manic and delusional or depressed and I easily lose track of where and when. So my recollection is not good as I have no idea where I am and when. Sometimes I am here or in the past or future, when I see people and places I have actually not seen or been to.

An early episode

Tanya my youngest daughter was aged between twelve and thirteen. She was aware of my illness and was a strong young girl who witnessed this incident and showed great courage when I had a manic attack.

I had lived in Murray Bridge for thirteen years. It was a rainy wet evening. My obsession began with drinking water, a lot of water, constantly, and I was listening to classical music. It was loud and I sang all day, flitting around the house. I just seemed to run through the house, from one room to another, like in my mind! And then out to the front yard and then the backyard. My children watched in disbelief.

'What the hell is up with Mum?' my son asked his sister.

This episode was a frightening thing to be witnessed by everyone. My family were confused and helpless and kept asking what was wrong. I ran into the lounge room where all the children and my nephews and friends were. The fire was roaring and I picked up a huge tree stump and held it above my head like King Kong! God knows what I was going to do with it.

My kids just stood in awe of it all while my nephew, who was lying beneath me, called out to me, 'Aunty Doris, what are you doing?'

I looked at him and put down the tree stump and took off.

By then, Jennadene had called my closest friend Margaret, who is like a sister to me. We had grown up together in Colebrook Home. As I ran around the house opening and shutting doors, Jennadene, John and Margaret were looking for me. I was like an escaped bird, fluttering endlessly around the house with my family trying to catch me and subdue me.

Margaret rang for the ambulance. I needed medical attention as my behaviour was not manageable at home. I was so unwell. I hid in my bedroom and ending up climbing out the window as Margaret and Jennadene watched my barefoot *chinna* disappear behind the house. I was running barefoot through the rain towards the waiting ambulance in my nightwear.

The ambulance officer was all official and thinking of strategies to corner and restrain me with the least amount of stress. By that time, I had tricked him in to thinking I had ran out the back door. Ahah! But I had gone through the front window and headed to the ambulance, climbed inside and made myself comfortable on the stretcher. I crossed my arms over my chest and closed my eyes as if I was deceased.

'Mum!' called Jennadene.

I then apparently looked down at my legs and commented that I hadn't shaved them. Jennadene stood totally confused and worried and told me my legs were fine. Meanwhile, the rest of the family were still looking for me.

It seems quite funny and raises a good laugh at the table when we recall it now. There I was on the stretcher while some were racing around looking for me, including the ambulance officers.

'There she is,' shouted my daughter.

I was totally unaware what was happening. I was in another world.

I was then transported to Murray Bridge Hospital. On my arrival, I became annoyed and lay on my stomach clutching a pillow, sounding out the letters on the eye test chart on the wall. 'A-E-I-O-U' repeatedly. 'Where are you, Thomo? About fucking time, Thomo!'

I was referring to Dr Thompson, who was on duty, as he walked into the room to assess me. He then swiftly recommended admission to Glenside Hospital.

This was the beginning of my journey with my psychotic episodes, my whole body accelerated at such speed physically and mentally.

It is a beautiful and wonderful world that I am in. I see things from a different perspective when I am unwell. I'm not aware of my own surroundings, they appear different for some reason. Bipolar mood swing disorder. Was that the diagnosis?

I had many visions on a journey, flying like a bird in the ambulance on the freeway. It was cold that night as I travelled from Murray Bridge to Adelaide. I knew all the roads and bends we took, though we were driving in darkness to Glenside. The ambulance was chilly and I was totally unaware that my daughter Jennadene was accompanying me.

I was swaying like the polar bears as we came down the Adelaide Hills and I even pissed myself as I was in this state of delusion and confusion. I was subdued but I was loud and called out to the ambulance officer and police officer who had accompanied him for safety. I knew exactly where I was going.

On arrival, I was placed in a secure observation room in view of my daughter and the nurse she was talking to. On several occasions I knocked on the glass window to get her attention.

She kindly told me, 'Soon, Mum. It's OK.'

'OK,' I replied, giving a wave like a kindergarten child in a play room.

Later I was happy to see my friend Barbara, an Aboriginal health worker. She arrived at the ward, which was unreal. To me, the ward appeared brilliantly lit with an immense white light and I could see her in the distance. Was I hallucinating? Did I see her in this brilliantly lit ward? Did I really see her? Had she arrived here all the way from Murray Bridge? The ward's brightness was ever so clear, crystal-clear like an angel bearing light on me and on Barbara. It was heavenly, spiritual. Was this an opening to a new beginning? This bloody dreadful and terrifying illness appeared with many dimensions.

Aboriginal women and connections

I have connected into another spiritual world of beauty. As a Ngarrindjeri *mimini*, my connections with the land and the seas and my culture are my foundation. This is delicate, but strong and important to me. This is how this connection emerged on one occasion.

My dear friend Mina and her youngest daughter and I decided to go to the beach to connect with the sea and enjoy the freshness of the salty water and air. The space was overwhelming. The lighting of the sunset was beautiful. We listened and chuckled with sensitive souls as we sat on the white sand. Feeling stimulated; our energy was high as we were captivated by the beauty of the sunset and what was around us. We sat sharing the moment, taking it all in so we would remember, as we did not have a camera that day to capture the sunset and the experience.

'Aunty,' a softly spoken voice called out to me, 'shall we collect shells to take home?'

Mina and I had time and space to embrace the beauty and time to heal and plenty of time to collect shells.

The ocean water gives us gifts and peace of mind to generate energy and strength with its significant connections to our spirituality. I refer to the Salt Water people. I recall seeing a documentary, seeing their survival and their means of living off the land and waters and what it meant to our Indigenous people.

We walked gathering beautiful coloured sea shells in the shallow salt waters. As the sunset was drifting in the distance it was beginning to slowly disappear through the coloured clouds, as it seemed to set to another world. The core moment of this was the connecting to the land and sea. The spiritual connection and healing was present for us both at this moment. In this time I found a deeper sense of belonging to my family, my culture, my language and my land. This occasion gave me strength and well-being, and created the urge to write. I am a leader to my family because I have had the courage to write. I have so many beautiful stories to tell.

Straw hat

Early on in my illness, I had become unwell again and was quite manic. Outdoors I wandered around as proud as could be. I had discovered a bushy shrub, one I liked. Creeping towards it, I crouched and crawled inside, sitting dignified inside this the bushy shrub, a shrub which was shaped like a *wurli*, and there I was, naked, feeling proud and wonderful. I was displaying my spirituality as a full-blood traditional woman. I was in full control and it seemed so real. It was real, and there I was in my own surroundings, demonstrating my Aboriginality, my culture, my land. I was absorbing the presence of my Ngarrindjeri spirit. To me at the time I was not hallucinating: I was in my healing environment. Then in that moment I was snapped back to reality.

'Doris! Kungka! Come inside before the police come!' called my sister Margaret with much concern and embarrassment.

At the time, she was on the phone to my daughter Jennadene, who was listening to everything. I emerged from the garden shrub of my Adelaide home, donning a bright yellow, red and black straw hat. Naked like my forefathers. My native land, my *wurli* was merely in the boundary of my front garden.

Strength and energy

I reach out through my writing with reverence, with understanding.

All races can suffer with grief, hunger, dispossession and identity crises.

I have the strength in my soul and hear their painful voices.

I endeavour to keep my culture strong. My history and the future generations need to survive with pride and dignity.

My energy expands with the vast perimeters of my dreams.

The gift of bipolar

When I become unwell, there have been times when it can be quite enlightening for me.

I recall a patient in the ward who became anxious, pacing the floor expressing his feelings aloud saying, 'Bipolar is a gift.'

The ward was restless and the patient had become quite boisterous and loud. Bipolar was a gift? So does that mean I am gifted? I was a gifted child, a child who was stolen by the government in 1945. A gift is given. So this was given to me, but by whom?

My child

We are the children who were taken away
Torn from our mothers' breasts.
Where is the guiding hand a child is meant to have?
The day I was conceived, life began.
The nurturing began.
I was surrounded by love, protected in my mother's womb.
The sense of bonding was all around.

The illness is like this

My feelings are markedly enhanced as I visualise the purity of the ice. The landscape of the snow where the bears roam brings me to understand the spiritual connections with the land and the seas from the peace, love and purity. Poland/polar? I can't explain why I have this association with the bears. All I know is it was brought on by bipolar. Bipolar = two polar, two bears. It is now a symbol for me, also likened to the saying, 'Bear in mind'.

I haven't been to many counsellors to help me through my struggles with my healing program. It has been a long and lonely journey for me to consider healing. Not too many people want to help or try to understand the trauma that many people have had to go through as an individual with mental illness. My personal experiences have been frustrating for me, as I have been often been misjudged on occasions about my behaviour. As far I was concerned, my behaviour was quite normal. Then I would be reminded, 'Have you taken your medication?'

I still have a lot to learn about this illness and what causes it. I strongly believe that it is not a hereditary illness. I lived in an institution for the first sixteen years of my life, alone and displaced with no family connections. I was in and out of bad relationships.

My children and my illness

In my hardest times, I remember when Tanya, my youngest daughter, gave me a beautiful pair of white doves to place in my shade house. To me it was a gesture of peace and love. I accepted the two doves with forgiveness, amusement and sadness on Tanya's part, I guess. I immediately reflect on the two doves who strive with innocence like the two bears, striving to survive.

I sometimes find myself in a manic state or a deep depression where I cannot motivate myself to do the simplest chores. Being with my family helps me in coping with chores and keeping active in the community. I do suffer horrendously with my downswings. I fear being ill, as it can be so frightening and frustrating. The deep depression is like being swallowed into darkness. My family is important to me because I can rely on them to support me when needed and on occasions share and laugh at the antics I recall of my past delusional, manic episodes.

I appreciate my niece Rosalyn, my sister's daughter, popping in for a visit from time to time and to assist me with the découpage, with the clippings of Aboriginal art from books and calendars that I have collected over the years. I was turning a table that I retrieved from John's home into a beautiful object for the entrance of my home. I like to keep myself busy with doing different crafts at home by myself or with groups that I attend in the community. I am proud that I love to give my makings away as gifts to my family and friends.

When I am unwell, I always look to go and live with Jennadene or have my son John stay with me to take care of me. I am rigid with fright in depression. I am always asking Jennadene if I can come and live with her and stay in the sleep-out, for her to look after me. I see she cannot burden herself, as she as one of her five sons in the sleep-out.

She says, 'Mum, every time you get sick, you're looking to stay with me.'

She knows that when I recover I love my own home and space. I do realise now I need my independence for survival.

Family relationships

I believe that I have been helped through rebuilding and connecting with my family, especially with my older sisters. I had to learn to go on this long journey through the traumas of searching many miles to be subjected to horrendous, painful and sometimes beautiful memories to come to where I am now.

Doreen, my eldest sister, taught me to be strong just by being there. I cry inside and then weep as I write this book. I continue to rebuild my culture based on what I have learnt about the past from Doreen. Through her study of Aboriginal life and families she has gained knowledge that is her great contribution. I said to Doreen, 'You are my bionic sister, a powerful woman, whom I look up to with the greatest respect.'

My whole family, particularly my immediate family, have helped with the understanding of my heritage, culture and language. This determination has helped me in rebuilding my life. There were times when I convinced myself that I did not have this illness, but instead had a broken spirit and believed that I was misdiagnosed as a sufferer of bipolar mood swing disorder. But it was not just a broken spirit.

Effect on the family

I don't remember any arguments about me being admitted to hospital during my illness.

When I ask Jennadene what I did, she says, 'It's all right, Mum.' She used to say that to me when I was in hospital. 'You're all right, Mum. It's all right, Mum. You've done the right thing, Mum, coming to hospital. You're being looked after well.'

I remember that my kids were really compassionate and loving to me when I was sick. But it's hard for children when their mother has a mental illness, with mood swings. What would they be thinking? Shame? Fear?

That time over twenty years ago I'm sure it was confusing and scary for them. Nobody knew anything. I didn't know anything about what the hell was happening to me. John would have been seventeen, and Tanya would have been twelve. She was twelve and had a mother with mood swings.

I remember an occasion when I lived in Murray Bridge, a Tudor-style house with bay windows. The front and back yards were huge. God! I remember I was digging out in the front garden. Suddenly it was a hole and I had dug it all out. It was big, it was huge, a huge fish pond, I thought. It did turn out to only be a hole, even though I thought it would make a nice fish pond that would be good for the kids. I thought, even a swimming pool. But it all got filled in. I did the digging, but the pool never happened. The kids didn't seem interested. I must have been on a high. That might have been the beginning of my illness, in Myall Avenue.

Family

In Murray Bridge, every day was a battle: learning my culture, my language, raising my young family This was when my father was alive and my two older brothers. My mum had passed on. I was in shock and never shed a tear. But my mother was with me as I travelled.

Manic episodes

I am not well again. I begin to race through the house. I see faces, many Aboriginal children's faces. I have admitted myself to the hospital. My Aboriginal spirit is evident and racing as I pace the floors of the ward. I go outside and sit on the ground with my people. I get up and dance with them until I begin to tire. But I am in a safe place and I finally rest my head in the early hours of the morning.

I remember following the red direction line in the corridor leading me to the outside. I recall saying out loud, 'Words are just like stepping stones to lead you on your way.' I paced the floor up and down saying this repeatedly.

On another occasion it is again time to pay a visit to my doctor or have a stay at Woodleigh House, the psychiatric hospital, until I get well. At the time, I find it hard to comprehend on what is happening mentally and physically. It was the same old thing, racing around the house from room to room. This time, I hid myself in the toilet. I'd also put all my pillows in there and had been trying to sleep. I ran in, squatting closely to the toilet bowl – I was hiding from someone or something – and then I raced down the hallway of my house.

Wires! *Nukkin* (look). I noticed the wires immediately. A coil of wires was leading from a reel and trailing through my lounge to my speakers. I honestly thought I was being recorded by a television crew: cameras – the whole bit. I was a noble Aboriginal woman with my loyal dog by my side that appeared to me as a dingo.

I had also taken pictures off my wall and any other items and stacked them in a pile in the centre of the kitchen table. At random I would pick something up and place it on the pile. On this occasion, a doctor was called to do a home visit. He was very patient and waited for an opportunity to inject a needle. He literally sat on me to inject me in the hope it would calm me down. I was calling out all sorts, not really making sense. I went by ambulance to Woodleigh House at Modbury Hospital.

More manic attacks

Sometimes, bipolar feels like a disease that eats my brain. Bad thoughts come into my head and eat my brain with confusion and madness. It's a terrible feeling, interfering with that brain. It's like a channel, like lines going through my brain, and you can't function throughout the day because it's all mangled. When my brain's been like that and I've been in bed and try to get up, I can't get up because I can't think. So I get back into bed and try to get up again, and I just can't. It's shocking, I tell you. It's terrible. How many times have I tried to get out of my bed and I can't? It destroys my well-being, my survival and strength, and I feel vulnerable.

When I am manic, I become creative. Although I have always been creative, I do become more sensitive and get obsessive in my writing. I cannot comprehend or eradicate my thoughts at the beginning of my manic attacks. I move at an extraordinary pace. Mood swings disorder comes at times when least expected.

I had raised my hands high with a jump to welcome Tanya and Jennadene on their entering the psychiatric ward at Glenside Hospital – just like the car advert on television: 'Oh, what a feeling, Toyota!' I was playing table tennis with another patient while others played eight ball. I wasn't allowed to play eight ball because I kept lying on the table and posing like Jesus on the crucifix. Somehow when I get ill, religion emerges.

I strive to do what I need to do, not running around like a headless chook, racing to the pace of the cars and what the world is coming to. I am concerned about the weather changes around the world, the lack of water and how the ozone layer is affecting us all and all God's creatures great and small.

Mood swings

I find my mood swings are literally swings. Like a pendulum. The whole picture of manic bipolar disorder is magically becoming unwell then well again. The mood swings are in themselves journeys of pure hell and sudden beauty.

When the days are getting shorter and winter has arrived, my mood changes, like many normal people with seasonal affective disorder (SAD). Our brains are affected by millions of pieces of information. I tell myself, 'Take heed and listen to your heart as you go from one mind to another.'

I have misplaced my written work. I bring to mind episodes of mood swings that have happened in the past. I write with unsteadiness of two occurrences, where I try to undress on the lawn at my niece's house, sitting with my legs crossed, with my niece trying to stop me as she tried to reassure me. I also distinctly remember the time of stripping off my clothes sitting under a shrubby bush in my front yard adjusting leaves as my pillow.

I become manic again, with my children taking me to hospital. I arrive at the hospital giving my details, talking loud. 'What bipolar? The two bears?'

The slip of the tongue can get me into trouble at times with the highs and lows. In the highs, I'm traveling at an incredible speed going north, west, east and south, and I am in my own space with so much to do. The dirty dishes pile up on the sink. There's washing to do, floors to be done, and the dusting. But nothing gets done. I only get into a bigger mess with my thoughts getting mangled, losing things. The keys I can't find, nor my glasses. I watch myself. Am I going mad? Can I get my brain into gear and start again? I not only misplace things, I put things in the most peculiar places. I question myself and swear I saw these things. My mind is playing games with me. It is so active. Where is my bloody watch? I saw, I saw it there. I search to no avail, thinking that I am hallucinating. I become stressed and sit with a cigarette. Bingo! I may find the watch days later.

    I have to adjust in my mood swings, to the feelings of low and high – just like the two bears – generating energy for my own self-esteem through the lows and the highs. Depression can last for months, making life like a trash bin of mangled metal. And I try to get myself out of that spiral of mangled metal as life goes on.

An early mood swing

It is July 2003. I have found it most difficult to continue with my writing for several weeks. My ability to focus on my writing is disrupted with my mood swings. I struggle to put words to paper. The weather is dull with dampness and rain and I have noticed that I have been immensely slow in my thinking. This is so upsetting as I become aware that I have experienced a mood swing.

I can cope with isolation but the ignorance of the community and people in general can be frustrating. I build trust with friends and frequently tell my history of illness with laughter or almost in tears and with nervousness.

The weeks of depression have had a hold of me as I ponder through each day. The housework is neglected. A shopping spree is upon me when I am on a high. The mood swings come and go as I experience a journey again on a roller coaster. This is damaging to my well-being, eating away my way of thinking.

At times, my feelings are not shared because of retaliation that I may or may not receive from my friends. It is a subject that is not discussed openly. There are other times when I can bring it up in a casual manner, 'Hey, I'm not well. I can't write.' I then have to force my energy to repossess my spirituality that has been taken from me. It is a damn curse to have the emptiness in one's soul.

I sit in the ward of Woodleigh House writing. I had to be admitted with this mood swing disorder. My son had come to visit me; he told much later that I was screaming for my mother. 'Where's my mother? I want my mother?' This had a great effect on John, seeing me in this condition and hearing me screaming for my mother. This is embedded in John's mind for the rest of his life.

I was fortunate to have visitors, but there were times when I couldn't remember them coming, or anyone coming. My sister Doreen had come to see me. She was shocked to see me in that condition. I was on heavy drugs and shuffling around the ward. I was not aware of her presence. This was disturbing for Doreen to see me in this way and she had a few words with the staff instructing them that I did not need to be taking so many drugs.

The positive healing treads through my frame of mind as I think of the two bears who stroll with their heavy padded feet into the snow with pride, with anticipation, a motion of sluggishness on the journey to their destination. Are we going back to an ice age? Is our weather changing?

I am sitting at my desk tapping my fingers believe it or not, listening to rap music. I don't normally like it, I chat to the patients, become friends and sit outside to smoke endless cigarettes. I listen and at times eavesdrop to learn and to be social in trying to counsel. Aat the same time this helps me make friends.

It has been difficult to even spell my own name or say where I come from, but I'm learning because I want to. At times I can pronounce it quite deadly as it is my language.

I begin to see things in a better perspective as write. I walked around the hospital ward many times. I would hum a couple of hymns and reflect back to Colebrook Home. 'Give me oil in my lamp, keep me burning.' Well that lamp is still burning and I am still shining.

Manic behaviour

Feeling elated and over-excited
insomnia, I sleep only a few hours
delusional
behaviour changes
obsessive behaviour
repetitive behaviour
increased strength and energy,
extreme irritability
rapid, unpredictable emotional changes
racing thoughts,
flights of ideas
increased interest in activities,
overspending
inflated self-esteem
poor judgement

Bipolar writing

'Bipolar all the way from Poland' is a humorous phrase that I can laugh and cry about when I am under control. Then I can write with strong views, telling my story with an amusing and clever attitude. But I need to be able to express my feelings no matter what mood I am in. If I was on a high now, my writing would be quite erratic and might not make any sense. I would raise my arms with amusement, 'Bipolar all the way from Poland', as I tell of my journeys as a sufferer of this mysterious illness.

It has been a slow process for me to settle back into developing my skills as a writer to overcome this illness. Unfortunately I cannot predict my moods and hence I suffer when it becomes apparent that my mood is swinging. When I started writing, I had been occupied with meeting friends and being active in other areas to deal with depression. I decided not to have any counselling but to go on my own, to just persevere with it to convince myself that life is not bad. I would be drawn back with negative thoughts or no thoughts at all but function just on vacuity that occurred for many days.

This is my illness and I can sit alone in isolation not feeling sorry for myself but determined to beat it. As I write now, my spirit is lifted with perseverance. Maybe I needed the time off from writing, maybe I needed to gather my thoughts, time to journey into my soul to cleanse my thoughts by just taking time to meditate and be in control. I try moving my head in a motion, clearing my thoughts as I write. It has been a while since I have done this but it helps me with this great energy.

Manic attacks

I say in a blatant way that becoming unwell can be a fucking frightening experience as I seem to believe then that I am 'normal'. I can literally crawl around on the floor in my house with mangled thoughts as I journey, travelling at an extreme pace. I ring for help to the local police station and think I am talking to a policewoman that I thought I knew.

I don't know how I get through the struggles of manic attacks. I had a vision of being a traditional Aboriginal woman who has been stripped of her identity, power, and dignity. But afterwards I am here to tell my story, a woman proud of my Aboriginality with a strong culture and importantly my own identity, a mother of three with many grandchildren.

March 2004 has been a difficult time for me with my illness upon me. I am experiencing deep depression. I am not functioning too well because of this. I have to accept the downer which I call 'Broken Spirit'. I become frustrated as my mood swings change. My thoughts become dormant. My body becomes restless and exhausted. Anxiety has set in as I try to overcome my illness. Depression brings me pain and tears as I am locked in with anger and frustration. I swear with frustration. I seem to have no escape. I think I'd rather suffer the highs because then at least I am on a journey of sensitivity.

Dark and light

Do not hide in your darkness
Enter your feelings into your soul
Express your mind towards the light
Let your energy exhilarate to positiveness

Manic again

I become unwell again, quite manic. I wandered around my front garden and discovered a bushy shrub. I then moved slowly towards it and climbed into my wurli. I was naked, feeling proud sheltered under the bush. There was a feeling of reconnecting with my spirituality as a full-blood traditional Aboriginal woman. I was in full control. It seemed so real. It was real, and there I was in my own surroundings, demonstrating my Aboriginality, my culture, my land. I was absorbing the presence of the Ngarrindjeri spirit. At that moment, I was not hallucinating. I was in my healing environment.

Thinking back

On one earlier occasion, before I was diagnosed, I had been at my cousin's house back in the 1980s when I was living at Murray Bridge. I became aggressive and was put under a cold shower by members of my family. No one knew what was wrong with me. From one mind to another again. I became unwell.

One other time around then I was at the Lower Murray Nunga's Club (an Aboriginal organisation) and having a great fit of strength, I broke a solid wooden office chair. I eventually went to Glenside Hospital.

When my stay at Glenside had come to an end, I was sent home with Ida, an Aboriginal woman from the Aboriginal Health Service, who was waiting to see me. It was overwhelming for me. Ida treated me with great respect. Very few words were spoken, as I recall, as she drove me home.

There were many more bouts, in some of which I was hysterical, and I was also admitted to local and Adelaide hospitals. This mystery illness would later be recognised as bipolar disorder.

This is me

Journey with me through my dreams of sadness and suffering and pain,
to a world of illusion, confusion
with upheaval
thoughts of misunderstanding.
I am truly sane.
A new world has taken me in a manic or depressive state.
People do not recognise my hidden illness as I live one day at a time and wait,
learning and challenging each day as it comes.
From one mind to another is how my mind runs.
We lost our families, we lost our heritage. Where do we belong?
We hold our heads high with pride, walking tall with dignity in words
and in songs.
As I write, I transform into a new me,
I am healing as I write,
just wait, you will see.

Being stolen

As a member of the Stolen Generations, I have suffered greatly in my life. This can be attributed to the injustice done to me and my experiences as a member of the Stolen Generations taken as an infant from hospital when my mother had died. I was taken away from my family when I was twenty-eight days old. I was denied the right to be with the rest of my family, with my siblings, my father, grandmother and aunts. As a member of the Stolen Generations, I experience upheaval, trauma, emotion, pain. How dare they take and interfere with the integrity of my Aboriginality, causing division and general apathy? I was denied my language and my identity and I received injustice.

My mother, whom I never knew, nurtured me with an abundance of love. Both my mother and father loved me. Any parents love their newborn children. But I felt unloved. I searched for love. I knew my mother loved me but she died of complications when I was only a month old. Sister MacKenzie took me away from my nanna and father. My nanna wailed for me for months. My dad searched for me for months but they wouldn't tell my family where I was. Doreen threatened to jump off the monument in North Terrace if they didn't tell my family. Doreen was looking after me. She was ten years and I was twenty-eight days old. Then Doreen was sent to Fullarton Girls Home and I was sent to Colebrook in Eden Hills.

My worst experience of my life occurred when I was growing up and I was told that I had another family, a family that I did not know, another family as well as the 'family' I had in Colebrook. Who? Where?

I got to know my own family when my father and brothers and sister visited me at Colebrook. It was after I left Colebrook that I got to know my family better. Thinking about my family also involves carrying with me for the rest of my life what happened in the past. There was no sign of mental illness in our family. I suffered in connecting with my family finding my brothers, sisters, cousins, aunts and uncles and nieces and nephews.

Doreen and my family experienced hardship at Raukkan, Point McLeay, particularly when I was stolen from the Murray Bridge Hospital. Connie was just three years old. This bought sadness and anger for my family. My father was a strong man but he had to search for me.

I continue the grieving for my mother and the loss of my family. I fill my mind with thoughts of hopelessness. I will follow your dreams, Mother dear: the bond is shared by two. I was protected by you for nine wonderful months. My protection shielded me from all pain, hate and cruelty. I was part of you, Mother dear.

The seasons

The seasons affect all people, all walks of life. The changes in weather bring mood swings in the society, and winter can contribute to depression. Feelings of disillusion with and mistrust of our leaders affect many people in different ways. It is time for me to pull the reins in, to be in control of my illness and to protect my well-being. We have to think positively to deal with the core issues of the times of injustice that have manifested throughout the world.

Medication

I was not sure then what was happening to me. I was pretty naïve and badly informed. All I knew was that I have a chemical imbalance in the brain and that I was taking numerous medications to control the mood swings. I recall once when I was sitting in a single lounge chair I had this wonderful feeling my body opening slowly through a tunnel of light. Then I came back to reality, feeling better in myself, with my medication working, a feeling of being reborn and a lift of resurrection. The feeling is astounding. It's hard to explain – it's a feeling of seeing a light at the end of the tunnel.

One for the highs, one for the lows, one for sleeping. It seems I have had an endless combinations of old and new drugs. Lithium is the main one, like the battery which needs to be recharged. Let the light shine in. Lithium keeps me on an even keel, evenly balanced to operate a normal balanced life just like anyone.

Another drug was Haloperidol. I remember Jennadene's friend Anne telling me this drug was very bad and not appropriate. She had been hospitalised as a teenager and treated with it. She also has bipolar.

When I was taking Haloperidol, I thought I had my arms bent over my head, with my body all twisted up. Was I hallucinating? Did it happen? My children said I was like a zombie, wondering around the house, in and out of rooms, my eyes wide open, with my children hoping that I was getting better. A person with mental illness may have periods in their life when they don't know whether what they thought happened had actually happened. What is real?

Most patients wouldn't know what medications they were taking. I did have some bad side-effects with some medications which made me feel that my whole body was twisted and my arms awkwardly positioned as I tried desperately to walk. It was scary as it gave me a sense of dying. Bipolar all the way from Poland.

My thoughts travel from one mind to another. I'm manic at this time, but I am in control, pulling the reins in. Later I am on an even keel, taking my medication religiously. Sometimes with confusion and racing thoughts, I stand in the kitchen wondering if I have taken my medications. Taking my medication helps me to be in control and to stabilise my mood swings and to relax me. It can become frustrating and frightening when I can't remember whether I have taken my medication.

Mental illness is deep! Our thinking happens in either state of mind. Ignorance or not, my illness needs to be managed and controlled by medication. My routine of medication reminds me of this every day. My lows or highs can strike at any time. However, I do have many good days.

Each day, I get frustrated and search, fumbling for my medication. I am normal as I stand with the pantry door open wondering if I have taken the bloody things. There would be many times that I have never taken them. And I am still here. I keep in control when things become a little dysfunctional, but it can be scary when you have this illness. Many times I had to discipline my mind my body and my soul and I have been administering these toxins for eighteen years. Have they been beneficial?, I am looking for alternative healthy arrangements.

I have been diagnosed with this terrifying illness and coming to terms with it has made me stronger in awareness about the illness. Acceptance plays an important part just like any other illnesses. As I focus on my well-being, I become vigilant about what the future is for me. I question myself about whether there is a cure, or can my illness really be managed with medication and the support of my doctors, families and friends?

Along the way, I had to be put through dreadful experiences of suffering painfully, spiritually, with bad side-effects from medications. I recall the effects during these experimental stages. I would feel nausea and vomit, have joint pains and feel quite disorientated, with muscle spasms and great discomfort. My whole body was being twisted, with my neck falling to the one side of my body and twisted arms in the air. I will never erase this memory of my experiences in a main public hospital in Adelaide.

Finally I am on the right medications but I do wonder how many people have experienced bad side-effects. I battled to feel human again as my medications were adjusted to get me stable enough to function as a 'normal' person. Today is what matters. Thirty years of my life have been controlled by medications. As I write, tears fill within my eyes, as I think of the wasted years and of the trials and tribulations of being controlled by medications whose name I sometimes cannot pronounce. I have had many tablets to drug me, so at times I cannot think, let alone try to work within own house.

The situation of bipolar patients

There is still not enough awareness about mental health. I believe people in general accept the illness but some see it as a taboo and just label us as if we are mad. Thank you, my friends. I am not ashamed of having this illness and I make it known, telling all my friends that I have already made it public that I suffer with bipolar. As a joke I mention bipolar, all the way from Poland, but it is no joke when I am manic. I have no choice. I do need treatment and have to go to hospital whether I want to or not.

I am a witness to poverty, greed and selfishness, seeing breakdowns in families for so many reasons, such as the lack of communication. Communication is so important as we strive or just try to live, adjusting to constant changes in the wide world. As bipolar sufferers, we live life in what seems a parallel world which can be horrific and unbearable. People with mental illness are not to be judged like we are poisoned by our own negative thoughts. These can be damaging with dreadful costs. We are sufferers, we are the consumers, and we should be able to discipline our frame of thought to beat this illness. The most important aspect for us is to overcome the stigma surrounding our conditions and illnesses. Then we will have the ability to leap the many hurdles of the illness. We get strong by accepting who we are and not looking for pity.

The struggles as a sufferer of bipolar disorder bring me to this conclusion: to accept my illness. I needed to educate myself about my psychotic episodes. However, it is sometimes difficult to perceive my illness, to recognise it.

Like the two bears, I continue with my history of bipolar illness that swings in motions just like the bears. My mood swings should be treated with understanding and people should be sensitive and understand our needs. Our voices should be heard with acceptance. Come with me on a spiritual journey, with the silence of peace and love like the two doves, connecting with me, for my well-being and my immediate family's well-being. Join my heritage and be part of my healing.

More history

What I had to endure in in my life time has sculpted me to who I am now. I was isolated, with no guiding hands. I went from one institution to another. Where was the guiding hand a child is meant to have? The upheaval in my teens and later in my life caused destruction of confusion and I believe this caused traumatic stress, but not bipolar.

As a member of the Stolen Generations, I had to nurture myself, dealing with the upheaval of being taken away from my family. This was the beginning for me– the stress of searching, connecting, learning my culture and in general learning of other cultures in this country. I believe that I may have developed my bipolar in the Colebrook Home. I used to curl myself up at the head end of the bed and rock myself to sleep with my comfort pillow. It was my baby.

I cried so much that the other kids called me 'Sooky' and teased me. Sometimes I would just take it, and sometimes I would run to the superintendent and beg her to stop the other kids teasing me. My anguish began with the continuous teasing. 'Canary! Canary! Sooky! Sooky!' I used to lie in my bed and rock that pillow and I still do till this very day.

Once when I was hanging out the washing, pinning up the clothes, I had an extraordinary experience that reflected back to my early childhood. I was a sooky sooky sooky baby. I see myself teary-eyed, as I stood, washing dishes, both at Colebrook and doing domestic jobs, as I worked for the ministers' home. I was so vulnerable; I am still and I always have been. I believe that it all started as a child – so vulnerable, experiencing horrendous changes in my life.

I struggled during adolescence and also later in life. I had suffered the pain of losing my mother and my family. This will never be erased.

These sad memories, with the loss of my culture, heritage and language, created my illness. I live to survive and stride just like the bears in a world of confusion and upheaval. With dignity and pride, I move with an open mind from one mind to another to pass down a history of survival. Our histories are important and should be recorded for the future generations.

Camp Coorong

It's Tuesday night in April 2008. I often go to Camp Coorong near Meningie in South Australia for healing, therapeutic healing on Ngarrindjeri land, on my land. Here, groups can meet and learn about Aboriginal culture and it is a popular tourist destination; many people have gone to Camp Coorong for cultural healing. I am healing at this moment as I write. Come and join me with my healing. I will walk tall with dignity on Ngarrindjeri land, my land, my home.

Understanding the illness: 2008

Although I now have a better understanding of the illness, compared with the past, I still need to educate myself further. I need to be able to tell my story to readers and for them to understand the journey that I have endured as I try to cope with the highs and lows. You see, when I get high, I behave in an accelerated way, my mind races, my thoughts come in no order, let alone make sense. I don't sleep and have been known to be up twenty-four hours before being sent to bed by family. If they are not around, then I stay awake. One time, stark naked and not sure what I was rambling on about, I got up religiously every hour and struck a small brass gong in my living room. My daughter Jennadene had to once again put on my nightwear and put me back to bed.

At least I am learning to recognise the symptoms, to be able to admit myself to hospital with the frightening episodes of psychotic behaviour, when I feel 'too wonderful' or more than just 'wonderful'. I have taken a walk at three in the morning and walked up to eight kilometres to Modbury Hospital in this manic state, barefoot and in my nightie. I ramble and rave, making no sense to anyone but myself. I often laugh with my family at my little escapades. Iit helps and it heals.

I recall visiting a Dr Kate, who would ask me how I felt. Was I too wonderful or feeling just wonderful? Being manic, I get so elated. I can be on a high and euphoric, which is the feeling of feeling too wonderful.

By the same token, deep depression is upsetting both for me and my family. I am now in deep depression as I write. I have felt this way for quite a while now. I continue to write as it helps to keep me sane and enables me to stay stable while I work at being an author. Working on the computer does help. I write periodically with the mood swings. Depression is the hardest thing to deal with. I feel that I am completely locked in a cocoon or maybe a white hole governed by bureaucrats or white liars. I am idle, motionless, but I try to be productive in my own way, fighting to live a normal life. I try to not hide in the darkness.

I am usually alone when I experience the effects of bipolar mood swing disorder. I manage with difficulties as I struggle with my day-to-day tasks. I just need to take medication and monitor my feelings and look for indicators. Any kind of stress, good or bad, including grief, can alter my chemical imbalance and trigger severe mood changes. The whole world suffers mood swings. Mine just go to the next level. I worry and see things on a grand scale which the majority may not view like me, as the world crumbles with wars and disasters. 'If it's not bills, bills, bills, its pills, pills, pills.'

Depression

Change in eating habits
preoccupation with failure, with inadequacies
loss of self-esteem
feeling of guilt
excessive concern about physical complaints
decreased sexual drive
crying easily
suicidal, occasional homicidal thoughts
sleeping all the time

Me and my leaders

Our world is governed with leaders we must follow. I survive through the decisions that the leaders make – wars, discomfort for all people. I feel helpless, and as a citizen of the world I am helpless. I am fed up with decision-making leaders. We are being dictated to and they are poisoning our minds with all this crap, like wars, like pollution, like cloning and environmental issues.

And for me there is this safe place, my home. Here I can cope and try to be productive in my writing and my daily chores. I have been able to learn alternative ways of coping with the impossible and learning how to get involved in the community. I had to learn how to focus on my well-being and my family.

We have no power to control the leaders, but we have powers to be strong spiritually in our beliefs. We are all connecting to our inner spirit or soul in trying to feel complete and compassionate, to believe in what is real and what is not.

The hardest part of my journey is darkness. When it is upon me, it surrounds me with emptiness, with misunderstanding, when people become aware of my illness. I search for my soul, for my heart, as I journey into a world of confusion. My spirit is not broken: I survive.

Life is always a risk. We take in what we eat and what we absorb from the environment. The ocean, the atmosphere and the land are being polluted, destroying the human race, starting new diseases that I have never heard of. Is it the chemicals we use in our domestic ways? Is it our everyday living? What is happening? For global warming, the warnings are there, but why haven't we listened, to our hearts, to our spirits, to our souls? With this illness, these issues disturb me more than the normal healthy person.

I often ask myself why wars are happening. The images of people who are suffering with the scars of war take hold of me as I watch television. I have had an unspeakable life of dislocation with the loss of my family – indeed, this has been a different type of war. I feel like those I see on TV. I cannot comprehend and never will, I guess.

Shades of colour

Becoming psychotic means I experience shades of colours, light and darkness. In the lightness, I journey into a world with the sounds of birds and a vision of wonderful insight into my spirituality.

My displacement as a baby has brought an experience of reconnecting with my family and also my spirituality. I perceive a world that other people say is not real.

I had a visit to the doctor at Nukkin Warrin Yunti and I sat in the waiting room. A feeling of warmth came over me as I waited for the doctor. A beautiful experience occurred. Clearly I saw a man, a strong traditional Aboriginal man.

I stood up and was asked by him in a softly spoken voice, 'Where you from?'

I turned to him and replied with no hesitation, 'I am a Ngarrindjeri *mimini*.'

I turned again and he was gone. I feel it was a privilege to have this happen to me, to have this experience with a tribal man.

Looking for help

For those who are pessimistic towards every issue about mental health, we, the sufferers, have to deal with the illness most of the time in isolation, shedding tears and constantly being asked by friends and family if we have taken our medication. In our crisis of despair we are asked, 'Are you all right?' How many times I wish I could have answered 'Yes!'

Where do we turn for help? The mental health services are there but how does one get immediate help when in deep crisis? I have literally crawled on the floor looking for a bloody phone number, only to get the local police station to send for an ambulance. The sufferers live a life of pure hell trying to cope and not be overwhelmed with this illness on a daily basis with mood swings that some people cannot comprehend. Then you might be ridiculed by the public or you may receive compassion. Bipolar is a hidden illness that I may never understand but it can affect me at any time.

Having discussions with friends and families helps immensely and being involved in the community, interacting with people and neighbours helps with stability and self-esteem. There is mostly no follow-up after you leave the psychiatric wards. I find this disturbing. No support, no care. I live alone, so how could they possibly know if I am OK. No visits by a health worker just to see if I am managing.

Colebrook

Today with my family I visit the Colebrook site, the place where I was raised with many other Aboriginal children who were taken from their families. It is a place for healing, for connecting with my extended brothers and my sisters as I walk through the memorial. This is my space and a time to reminisce and to reflect on my extended family. This is precious time for me to heal.

I have got back my culture, my language, my heritage and my identity. I live with dignity and pride, enjoying my life to the fullest with my family and my grandchildren.

I journey into fantasies of dreams of hope and despair. I keep myself busy. I do talks at schools or visit the Colebrook site to do speeches about the Stolen Generations. This has helped me immensely in keeping my sanity. Aboriginals who have suffered with grief or loss of family of being stolen receive a lot of help in connecting with their culture, heritage and language. I am fortunate enough to be in a group called Link Up, a service that has helped many Aboriginal people to connect with their families.

The loss of my mother and being stolen has played a big part and I believe contributed to my illness. It has influenced me. I was distraught on learning of my mother's loss and on hearing how my family had suffered with years of the pain and shedding of tears without me. This illness that has taken me over, I believe it happened with the removal of Aboriginal children. And that should never have occurred.

Doreen

My sister Doreen, who has since passed on, came to see me. She was shocked to see me in the condition I was in, heavily drugged and shuffling my feet around the ward. In my state of mind, I was aware of her presence. It was disturbing for Doreen to see me in this way. She had a few words with the staff, instructing them that I was over-drugged and I did not need to be taking so many medications. It affected my children to see me in this state of confusion, a broken spirit. I was a feeble old lady in the ward. I was a woman who had standards, and here I was in this ward trying to find out who I am and what I am, what am I here for? Many times my medications were questioned due to the effect they had on me. My family could not understand why I appeared worse on the medications than without them.

I have learnt remarkably from Doreen, a woman with powerful strength to go on with her fight to stop the Hindmarsh Island bridge from being built. It was a horrendous struggle for her and her supporters as I watched and taped the media coverage on television.

John

I felt I was reclaiming my identity, my family and my heritage while I was admitted to the various institutions. When my son John first visited me in hospital, it was stressful for him to see me in that state. I can only vaguely recollect his visit due to the condition I was in. My upbringing, being one of the Stolen Generations, would also have had a great effect on him as my son. He knew of my suffering from the time I was a baby and when I was an adolescent and an adult, and now I was in hospital, sometimes reduced to being helpless by grief.

On one occasion I was being taken to hospital by health workers in a government car, when my son turned and said to his sister Jennadene, 'Poor Mum, she still being taken away.'

In hospital

On one occasion I was again high and needed to go to Nunkuwarrin Yunti, an Aboriginal health organisation. I strolled and roamed around the waiting area making connections with Aboriginal people and other ethnic patients and workers. I had entered the waiting room to visit the doctor.

The appearance of the circle of chairs in the waiting room seemed to trigger and bring together awareness and belonging. The medical staff were compassionate and were aware of my needs as a bipolar patient. Their response has also helped me to understand my need to belong in the community, being human and needing people. The circle of love and care is there.

Many times when I went to hospital I had no one with me, mostly due to the fact it was early hours and my eldest daughter lives in the country, over an hour away. My other children were unable to assist, having young children of their own or having no transport. I have learnt to deal with being alone. Where is the guiding hand the child is meant to have? I've learned to be strong and I cope.

Despite those long years of dispossession, of separation from my immediate family and culture, I am strong and I am holding my strength. This does enable me to laugh or cry through the experiences through my highs and lows. The process of just being hospitalised is not easy, but I get the picture.

To receive help, one has to go through the right channels no matter what illness you've got, though it is more frustrating waiting to see a doctor in a major hospital. Long hours of waiting, getting more restless by the hour. I remember getting up to pace. I then walk along the corridor following a red line directly to the outside. I walk around and pretend I'm on rocks and I chant, 'Words are just like stepping stones, to lead you on your way.' And look where the words have led me, on my way. I am in dire straits when I'm on a high, waiting to be seen. It was so painful just being alone.

Writing

I am an author and normally an outgoing person who enjoys space and the simplicity in life in general, gardening, cooking and hobbies, which are rewarding for me. The biggest achievement was the launch of my autobiography *Kick the Tin*. Since then I have moved on with determination to publish a children's book *Bush Games and Knuckle Bones*.

Now time has come for a new beginning. Armed with assertiveness and awareness of this illness, I can do what I enjoy most, writing and gardening. Each season brings new beginnings, new cycles and the simplicity of life. The hearing of birds, the pigeons cooing in the distance, the nature and smell of the garden give me great joy.

I write as I stride. My motion is just like the two bears. So join with me on my journeys with the generation now and for the generations to follow. Life is too short and I want to enjoy life to be able to tell my stories as a writer. As I write, I am listening to Enya then switch to Archie Roach, an Indigenous performer.

To keep the spirit alive as a writer I think of the two bears strolling with their heavy padded feet in the snow with pride, with anticipation.

I am always intrigued with words and like to practise by experimenting with words that I cannot pronounce. However, I am willing to learn words, to mess with words that confuse me. In doing this, I have learnt many words of my own language, my culture.

I find it difficult to write at times due to the mood swings and, coupled with poor education and the pace of technology, I do struggle to keep up. I also write for validation, for acceptance and to convey my need to express myself and to tell my story as a sufferer of bipolar.

As I write at six o'clock in the early morning, I hear the songs of the birds with the sun rising, giving me light. I enjoy the nature that is present in our beautiful, beautiful country. I appreciate the beauty, I hear the songs of the birds, and I am grateful for the light. Morning I find best when my brain is in gear to the sound of the birds and with the sun rising slowly.

It is hard even to understand what is occurring around me or even in my own space. There are challenges that we all face on a daily basis that are often taken for granted. I am sitting in this room, writing this damn book, all alone. I am alone. I am hearing nothing but the computer, hitting the keys of the keyboard. I journey on with the heavy task of dealing and coping with my illness.

Now I have found a deeper sense of belonging, to my family, my culture, my language and my land. This has given me strength and wellbeing, strength to accept the urge to write. I am a leader to my family because I have had the courage to write. And I need to keep a good frame of thought to beat this illness. The most important aspect for those of us who have this illness is to overcome the stigma of our diagnosis. Then we can understand how to leap the many hurdles of the illness. We get strong by accepting who we are and not looking for pity.

Many times, I struggle to write. I can't get anywhere unless I get started. I know that I have a difficult task to finish this book because of my mood swing disorder. I believe that I am strong and brave to tell my story. I share my experience with bipolar, and I meet other writers. I have learnt by listening to others. Sometimes they tell us that there are opportunities out there to grab and hold in being productive in what you have. Writing, I am taking an opportunity to grab and hold what I have – the experience of bipolar.

As I battle with this book, its task seems huge at times, but it gives me the opportunity to share. I have input from friends who have had personal experiences with mental breakdown. I do fear being labelled with this dreadful illness and I hope mental illness will be accepted more in today's society as it has been acknowledged in the younger generation.

I believe that keeping active and having determination do contribute to our well-being and survival. I spend time away from home escaping to my sister's place in the country at Point Pearce. There, I write and wallow in the peace and stillness. I write in the early hours, hearing the possum scratching in the walls. The determination in my blood brings me solace as the morning sun rises. In solitude, the morning sounds of the birds bring a new day of appreciation.

My awareness has contributed to my gift as an author. I see that being able to write is a gift given to me. I write in simple terms, writing in silence. I am pursuing this illness. I have the strength in my soul to heal the pain. Now I have found a deeper sense of belonging, this has given me strength identity to keep my pride and dignity in my well-being. My energy expands with dreams through my writing. To write and to reconnect, to accept I am a leader. I have had the courage to write this book.

I don't know that person

As I have said earlier, I see things in a different perspective when I am unwell, which can be incredibly confusing for me. People's names and faces emerge. I see faces, familiar faces, but I don't know that person. I hear names, I know the names, but I don't seem to know that person. The names tie in with the names of people I know, but I don't know this person. I try to figure out what is happening to me. I try to identify the many faces that seem to be familiar to me as I walk through the shopping centres, buses or malls and walkways. They are faces I don't know so I hesitate to approach them, saving myself from embarrassment in the nick of time. At times, I find my writings on the table, pages and pages of it. I write on everything and anything, notepads, envelopes, scrap pieces of paper, mostly names and words that either rhyme with the name or something spiritual or words that are triggered by that name.

Today is a *Bran Nue Dae* (which is a play from Broome by Jimmy Chi). I say this often. I perceive instant memories as I recall my visit to Derby to visit an extended auntie and her husband. I smile as I write with the deepest respect. I just love *Bran Nue Dae*; a brand new day brings spiritual beginnings.

The battles of mental illness

I am fighting a huge battle, coping with my medication. The problem I still face is not having ongoing support from doctors or maybe counsellors, but I think I have overcome this by writing and being with positive people. Doctors can be supportive in some ways but they are often only quick in instructing me to take medications.

I'm also outraged at the government mental health system and why the institutions are closing down. This is destroying the lives of many people who suffer with mental illness. We do not want to live as second-class citizens because of our being labelled and stigmatised, just as I surely lived this as a Stolen Generations Aboriginal woman.

Do these two stories have similarity, or has my mind become haunted by my past, or am I revisiting the past only to be locked into my present? I am in a time machine.

Mental health

We need to seek alternative measures as a nation to live normal lives with dignity and pride. We live in a world of destruction demonstrated by wars, violence, crime and environmental issues. We are confronted daily via the media. When destruction happens on a large scale such on September 11 and in tsunamis, it impacts worldwide on each individual in a negative way, leaving us feeling powerless to act. I feel in a vulnerable position on hearing so much coverage of these events. I find much of the news needs a shock absorber like a car, because it can be disturbing to any person who is suffering with mental illness. I cannot reconcile what I have to absorb as a human being. The disturbing news affects all walks of life. We can be brainwashed with negativities.

My attitude towards mental health is that not enough is done. There are people who are damaged emotionally and spiritually. Our lives are obscured with complications in everyday life, with bereavement, family breakdown and trauma that confronts us, housing and health. The biggest downfall that I have seen is that if people are not properly housed it can cause further frustration.

Having conferences and open discussion and continuous meetings does not help. There is no follow-up with patients who are desperately crying for help. People are sent out to live in the street or housed in confined units with poor health, where I wouldn't allow my dog to live. The conditions are appalling: there is drug abuse, alcohol abuse, so where are the workers? And what is the government doing about it? It saddens me when I hear these stories. Patients need to have visitors to chat to and give them that sense of empowerment, independence and have some say and input in the mental health services. I found being unwell I had the feeling of humiliation, of feeling shame so that facing people was difficult.

Money and mind

I often saw myself as a victim. Money and greed can be a root of all evil and with my illness I have spent money carelessly. I go to the hotel to gamble my money, and then, full of guilt because of squandering the money, I try and double it. Sometimes a small win, sometimes I lose the bloody lot. Then I feel sick because I have spent my food money. This has made me feel so bad, but life goes around like a roller coaster. My thoughts seem to come from one mind, then from another. Where is the guiding hand a child is meant to have? Eventually I have taught myself to budget and only take the minimal amount of money to a game that I do enjoy.

The younger generation

My concerns are also for the younger generation who are experimenting with drugs. I have experienced their effects within my family, community and my people. The drugs confuse their brains. Often kids are taken away, placed in foster care, once again 'stolen'.

Stress and drugs also have a major impact on Aboriginal families, causing upheaval in our social structure. Peer pressure – a new term that I have learnt, contributes to alcohol abuse, followed by drugs such as glue, solvent and petrol sniffing, or the heavy drugs like amphetamines. Big dealers are making the big bucks to feed the young people's addiction, causing destruction in marriages and relationship breakdowns. The dealers create social problems with horrendous outcomes for Indigenous and white Australians. I suffer a mental illness and I watch suffering that can be prevented. I wonder about my illness: could that have been prevented?

The seasons

Winter can affect the mood swings, making us feel low, and this contributes to feelings of hopelessness and adds to our mood swings. Winter can contribute to depression. This is known as seasonal affective disorder, SAD. Spring on the other hand brings life with the mood swings, moving us differently with feelings full of energy and high spirits. This brings a change. I'm feeling wonderful happiness and the need to go outdoors to do the gardening, to contact with Mother Earth, the worms, the soil, the bees and the honey. I remember doing a project on bees, on the making of honey, when I was a student at Eden Hills Primary School.

Managing my illness

I have become more open about my illness. Having discussions with friends and families helps immensely, as does being involved with community activities and committees. I still have a lot to learn but I can now manage myself a lot better. I can only learn by being me. Having contact with people who suffer with mental illness does help tremendously. I know there are people who are ignorant about mental health and who don't care or just don't bloody want to know about it and there are problems with people who suffer with bipolar some of whom cannot deal with it. Many of these people cope by administering their own medication and really struggle and are worse off than me. However, we are vulnerable as sufferers and many mental health patients can be taken advantage of.

The colour of laughter

We are not alone: the sadness has gone;
Laughter is here as we share our dreams,
A start of a new beginning.
Full of colour, we carry our laughter;
Let it be heard, for we are not alone with our wildest dreams.

A journey of healing

At the beginning of my life, I wore the words of 'Broken Spirit', the day of dispossession of my family. I have now connected to my roots in the Ngarrindjeri people, known nationwide as being subjected to dispossession. As an individual of the Stolen Generations, I was directed on a journey through my strong beliefs in spirit, connecting with my culture and many other cultures. Others of the Stolen Generations are on their way to healing, where they are endeavouring to find their cultures. I fight for justice and stability to tell my story and put my strong views on the Stolen Generations for those who have suffered numerous pains. My words and energy act just like the line in my first school primer book: 'Words are just like stepping stones to lead you on your way.'

I am on a journey of healing. Each day is a new day as I express my feelings in this writing, of connecting me with my family and the outside world. The outside is full of anger. Many changes in the world set the pace that we have to keep up to. We all struggle to keep our dignity, as I do myself as a human, as an individual Indigenous woman with this illness.

Dispossession

I believe in my heart I was dispossessed. Government policies had an enormous impact on our people. They stole me from my family. My grandmother and my father mourned for me for many months, mourned for their baby, for me, Mulparinni Doris Kartinyeri, stolen, a member of the Stolen Generations. As a babe in arms, I was placed in the care of missionaries employed by the United Aboriginal Mission. I was stripped from my culture, my family, my heritage and subjected to sexual abuse. Why did the Aboriginal Protection Board steal me from my family when I was just twenty-eight days old?

I have a broken spirit from losing all that I had in my life, my family, my culture, my heritage and my language. This I know within my heart – that I didn't inherit this illness and that one day I am going to slowly wean myself off the tablets.

Am I to believe that I have been misdiagnosed? Have studies been done by psychologists and social workers on children who have been taken or stolen from their families? Many Aboriginals are treated with medications or thrown into mental institutions on the grounds that they are mentally ill. It is the next generations that will be victims of injustice of the Stolen Generations. I had to start a new chapter in my life by searching for my family. This was a long journey. I had to adjust to fit in and reclaim my culture.

My culture

I am still learning when I revisit Raukkan and Camp Coorong and Coorong Wilderness Lodge. I keep active in learning Aboriginal history. Non-Aboriginal organisations have also helped me through their own interest in the Stolen Generations. They allowed me to write a poem for a gardening group on Kaurna land at Gilles Plains, sharing the Aboriginal culture. This has taught me to understand more about my culture and my family tree and again my extended families and of our Aboriginal origin.

Friends help the healing

Loss and grief, sharing, love and caring are words that are relevant for me today but my favourite word is 'inspirational'. Many friends have inspired me to continue with my writing. Today I am able to talk and share the experience openly about my journey, dealing with the anguish that I had to endure throughout my bouts of my highs and lows: just like the bears, High and Low. Part of my healing is sharing my illness with humour and with friends. Sharing and talking to friends about being manic, and having psychosis and depression, can relieve your pain and can make life easier. Having an open mind about mental illness can strengthen understanding and healing.

Being drug-free

Once, early in my illness, I was in a spiritual mood and influenced by a doctor to go drug-free. My heart was set to go drug-free. I vowed that I would rid all toxins from my body and live a normal life, drug-free. I had been invited to go to a day-long conference in Adelaide to participate in the Drug Free Program. It was my choice to go drug-free and I paid to hear about this wonderful program. I thought it would be good for my well-being and help others who have been diagnosed with mental illness. Unfortunately, it didn't work for me.

I was impressed with a program that claimed it would rid me of all the toxin in my body. It is difficult for me now to comprehend that I was advised and encouraged to go on supplements. I slowly weaned myself off my psychotic medications which I had been on for the last twenty years. What this did was destroy, in a matter of few weeks, all my efforts in dealing with my illness. I went ballistic again in trying to full-on cope with my illness, which was too severe for me to handle. My thoughts were racing, racing at such a pace I could not keep up. I had to be admitted to Woodleigh House.

I wonder how many other people have been trapped into contributing money and have followed me into feeling unwell again. There was no one to help me to bear the excruciating pain I went through as I went drug-free. I have learned now to listen to my body and to administer my medication religiously to control my mood swings.

I lost my culture, the white fella way

Let me fly to the destiny of drug free.
My broken spirit will be healed
I am me and you are you
Let me decide to go free to connect with my culture
I heal within and journey the road with guidance

More highs and the lows

In the highs, I feel extremely wonderful and my dreams travel to the east where the sun rises. The beauty begins, the birds are singing, the trees are shimmering in the light. I listen to my heart. Many wonderful visions take me on a journey. My movements may become erratic, and I may become boisterous and vocal. The extreme highs that I have experienced were wonderful. I danced to my surroundings, the birds and the trees became magic, my mind travelled through beauty. The vision is quite vivid.

I sat with my niece as she told me how, earlier, I sat with her on her back lawn, totally out of it. It was a hot day and I insisted that I sit in the hot sun. I was so unwell I began to undress and was prepared to sit partially undressed or naked. My niece had to get to her mother and take me home. Connie stayed with me at my house and decided to put a video on of her fiftieth birthday party, I became overwhelmed when I saw my brother. I wasn't coping and began to cry. She had to ring for Jennadene, my eldest daughter.

I have been in contact with friends and neighbours who have given me gifts. We seem to exchange gifts. Having this illness, I am vulnerable to giving things away, and people take you for granted. When I'm well, I then realise that I have parted with my prize possession. When I become well again, I also tend to make promises and not to stick to them.

I recall an incident when I was standing on my patio admiring native trees that I had planted. One, which I call my 'Colebrook Tree', had a great significance to me: it stood tall with its many branches. The story behind the Colebrook Tree had been told to me by Auntie Faith, an elder from Quorn. I was chatting to my son John. Oh! how wonderful was the tree as it stood tall and my thoughts danced. I am aware of everything around me. This was a silent moment of sharing with John, as we stood while I was in such a state of mind that I was at peace, admiring the beauty. Each branch represented something special as I was connecting the beauty of the tree. The roots of the Colebrook Tree represented all the families of Colebrook, and my family whom I have now found. The branches represented my children, the *tjitji tjuta* (the many children of Colebrook) and my extended family.

With bipolar, my mood is unpredictable so that I have to deal with it at any time and be prepared to be carried off in an ambulance to Woodleigh House. I need to be positive, as the highs and the lows can be frustrating. I am authorised to take my medications so I need to have my Lithium and Valpro to keep me stable: this helps with chemical imbalance in the brain, whatever that is. To top it off, I need to have blood tests every few months to keep records of the Lithium levels; I will become unwell again if the levels are too low. The medications can then be adjusted.

The sunset is so beautiful as I write. Wake up, Australia! Enjoy my view now! As I laugh, I feel wonderful most of the time and some people take it the wrong way when I may be a little over-excited. Have you taken your medication? I can become a little loud. All I want to do is live to the fullest enjoying my children and my grandchildren.

Later I will be dealing with tears and frustration with anger and hopelessness. The isolation kicks in, with depression bringing me pain and tears. At times, I avoid going to hospital as it is a long process to be admitted as a patient. I move in a manner with no control mentally, as I pace my house with resentment. I cannot escape the pain, I swear more often than I should. I try to avoid the phone while I am in this state of mind.

I then move to my computer. My home is my haven. I am fragile as I choke up with emotion, feelings of sensitivity overcomes me whether I am high or low. To disguise the high's high and the low's low is the hardest for me to deal with. I tend to misplace items. I seem to be in control and motivate myself to find the missing items and with great frustration. My housework is avoided; I at times find it hard even to make my bed. 'Who cares, only I live here.'

I sit here as I write with tears of despair, desperately trying to cope with this damn illness. I maybe a little high, with thoughts racing at a pace. I have not seen my doctor for a period of time.

It's just the beginning

Mother, you have carried me for nine wonderful months.
With your nourishment you have fed me with love;
You felt my kicks and movements which pleases you.
This bond is shared by two.
I was protected from all pain, hate and cruelty.
The slightest movement inside you told you
That it was time for a new beginning.
Our life together is shared with a bond that can never be broken.
I move with contentment feeling your presence as
You sing with laughter, your encouragement and
Tenderness I encountered every day.
My time has come to endure my new life
My movements have brought you pain.
Together we shared our lives.

Depression

I find depression the hardest to deal with. I feel more comfortable with being manic than being on a depressive journey. With depression, I am locked within, with no escape, my body has no soul, and my spirit is broken. I move with no emotions, no self-esteem, in isolation. It is just outrageous. The depression takes me over so that I feel that I am locked in a cocoon with no opening. I am at home completely isolated from the world. I have no one to assist me in showering or to dress or do my housework or yard. What does one do? I just lie in my bed, and wander around the home full of hopelessness.

How many people have been in this position, feeling isolated, and, heavily drugged, have not been able to communicate with the outside world? Many of our people are hospitalised due to depression and a breakdown of their identity, causing havoc within themselves by resolving their problems with alcohol abuse or illegal drugs. I have done my share of abusing alcohol, looking for a way out in searching for my family and connecting to my culture.

I feel depression is brought on from many things, such as trauma, loneliness and poverty, or family breakdown. If your life is dysfunctional and unbalanced, a crisis can cause upheaval and tragedy. Many a time, I have been frightened, petrified of not waking up the next morning. I feel no one should bear my anguish or share my pain. I have been treated with these medications not knowing what they were for and I do recall being locked in a padded room. I vaguely recall coming out highly sedated with little help from anyone. I do remember that I wished I had visitors. However, I may have had visitors and don't remember them. I do remember that my children did come to see me and they did manage to put a smile on my face.

I try to balance my mental scales and struggle from day to day as I write, and at times find it hard to focus. The weather is dull and wet. I'm not functioning and cannot cope with everyday life. I dread mornings, so I tend to sleep half the day, I become restless as I rise from my bed in one minute and then out with my feet. But with frustration I lie back down, curling myself up in bed. With the depression, I feel only parts of me are working. It's a terrible feeling. I can suffer with depression for three months. My whole body feels dormant. I cannot do the things I want to do. I have not been on my computer for three months to complete this book. I feel fragile with no energy.

The maniac depression plays a major part in my life as I struggle to choose what's best for me. At times life seems such a burden. I even struggle to do my housework. I cry instead of smiling or even laugh and cry at the same time. Depression does take a toll on me and I have no control. In all walks of life, I not only see it in me, I see it all around me, which can impose on my own well-being and I struggle to comprehend why?

How does one escape the illness? The isolation with the pain and learning to cope is an unbearable task for anyone. Life is an effort as I try each medication to prevent occurrences of my illness. It is my choice to have good self-esteem and to build my life positively. Manic depression is like a nasty word for me as I struggle to write now.

After the manic episode

I have come home. It takes me a while to adjust to my own surroundings. Being on my own in such a state can bring problems. After one manic swing, I destroyed my study room and my kitchen, with papers strewn throughout the house that came from my office. Where were the helpers? Here I was, sitting on the floor, out of control. It was early morning about five-thirty. I was in no state to look for friends' phone numbers, so in the end sitting on the floor I rang the local police station. I was quite manic and erratic, but I knew that I was unwell again by the time the ambulance arrived.

I managed to walk to the ambulance. I admitted myself to hospital. In the ambulance, I was again assessed. I hear myself reciting the books of the Bible, every book in the Old Testament. Who was looking after me? I asked for Auntie Lowitja as I moved and spoke to the doctor.

I have no control of the emptiness that has overcome my well-being. I had no contact to the outside world.

It is appalling that there is no follow-up with workers in the health department to converse with and just to see how I am. With the isolation and suffering with the chronic depression, one cannot help but feel unwell and to look up in the phone book to look for some help. We are the forgotten victims, penalised with an illness that is frowned on, an illness that we do not wish on anybody.

On the way up again

The lessening of my illness stirs me towards reality, with a need to perform actively in my surroundings. I begin to participate within the community and begin to write again. A long break from my writing doesn't help me, as it makes me feel inadequate within myself. It takes great courage to put aside all negative thoughts and those of the people who in any way influenced me in being involved with negative attitudes. I need to stay clear of negative people and focus more on myself and receive support from my close friends who carry positive values. This helps me immensely in reconstructing my life for surviving my depression.

There have been many times that I had to journey to take time to develop a method to have peace of mind. We all need to stimulate the mind, body and soul, whether it involves walking, doing sports or taking the time to perceive what is around us.

I listen to music for relaxation and I write. I enjoy Enya and contemporary or classical music and country music, so that, with the burning of candles, I can switch off from the outside world. This is my way of relaxing and having time to balance my thoughts and body and soul.

I enjoy writing, meeting people, laughing, joking about, as long as I don't get too excited, otherwise people will immediately think that I am unwell. For God's sake, I'm a human being with feelings.

When I do go into town, I tend to study people either on the bus or in cafés. Some faces will look familiar and I get a bit confused. Many faces look familiar while I am in the city – is that part of my illness?

I met up with two friends. I owed them both money. Money is no issue to me – easy come, easy go. It's nice to have friends who I can sit with and laugh and eat in an open restaurant. But at times doing this can feel that I am sitting in a pig farm with all the noise, the hassle and bustling of people, everybody sitting around talking while they eat.

Being active in the community

I have been productive in many ways in being active in the community. Throughout my times, I have been involved in community work and a gardening group, and been an Aboriginal education worker in visiting schools to tell my stories. The garden group that I am involved with helped me in setting goals. I keep busy and have a positive attitude and the support from my family. Life is a real challenge but I try to be active and involved in the community. I believe now in my heart that if you keep active the mind will reap rewards.

I live an active life and this has helped me to control my illness. I make myself available to various committees and I enjoy life today with my family and working in my garden. I keep busy in my local area. I enjoy my own space; therefore I have dabbled in painting for relaxation. I tried my skills in doing basket weaving at Camp Coorong, an art that has been passed down in the Ngarrindjeri culture. Basket weaving is a culture that connects. I have other hobbies. I have time out to help. In the gardening group, I was asked to write a poem. This was an honour and I accepted. The poem will be set on a rock and read by many people who visit the garden. Being active does help immensely.

I also visit the Colebrook site with family. This is my space and a time to reminisce and to reflect to my extended family. This is precious time for me to heal.

I am able to go to schools and colleges to talk about the Stolen Generations, though I am often still questioning whether I can cope in sitting with students. I have been to many schools with feelings of apprehension. But in the end I do have good memories on my visits to schools, sharing, answering questions, fulfilling my beliefs with every possible strength. Doing what I enjoy helps me to heal inside and forget my illness. It's a time to share my stories as a member of the Stolen Generations and to contribute and to teach the next generation.

My independence allows me to visit my friends and to get involved in community meetings when I feel up to it.

The world is perfect but not the people in it. There's wars, killings, murders, disasters everywhere. How does one survive with all this madness around us? Switch off the bloody television!

Looking at myself

My energy is generated by having many things to do, keeping myself being busy. Generally, I am flighty sort of person but I keep involved with what is happening in the community. I consider myself an outgoing person with many friends. I love to write and enjoy my space and the simplicity in life. Being productive has brought with it many achievements, especially with my hobbies. I enjoy cooking.

I sometimes believe that I have been brainwashed about my illness. I am as normal as my next-door neighbour. I see myself as a beautiful, intelligent and a gifted person who needs a chance in life.

My past has helped me to write my stories, stories that need to be told. My biggest challenge was my first book *Kick the Tin* that was my autobiography. This was a big success for me to write all that with my mood swings. But the struggles paid off. My childhood will never be erased as I write, even if I experience the odd mood swing. This gives me the strength and the power to write. I have a lot to offer, not just to myself, but to other sufferers.

Life is always a challenge and I am sharing my stories to pass on my strength and courage as a writer. We all have goals and this is mine. Never give up, no matter how bad things look. I get my inspiration in visiting Colebrook and sharing good memories with other members of Colebrook; the reunions and meetings lift my spirits. The memorial I visit flows with overwhelming joyfulness. I united with both of my sisters Doreen and Connie when we met at the Colebrook site. It was a big day for me and family, and as a sufferer of bipolar this showed me that stories being told and sharing can help in rebuilding your way of thinking.

My first television interview on a current affairs program with Mike

Munro was the most challenging and confronting issue that I had to deal with. However, it came across as I sat nervously and awkwardly being questioned about my book.

Friends with mental illness

A friend will ring, so I gather my things. It could be late at night so I will go to her house to comfort her and have a chat. One other time, I had visited her and her friend was with her, with everybody talking of their experiences at the hospital, or discussing their diagnosis and making mockery of the mental health system, laughing, swearing and carrying on as they drank liquor or smoked. The room became boisterous as I sat quietly drinking my coffee. I stayed for a while contemplating whether I should leave. These gatherings can help to a certain point but it can get to you. If you are not a strong person, you can become overwhelmed with enthusiasm.

I remember one year being with a friend on the day of the march for NAIDOC. We met at Elder Park. I was so pleased to see her. We sat and we talked. I spoke about my next book and the children's book. It startled her and all of sudden she became quite vocal.

'The whole world is suffering fucking bipolar, the whole fucking world is suffering with bipolar, look around us!'

I raised my hands with shame, and to hush her. In my opinion, she was right, but I felt a bit embarrassed that her voice was heard loud and clear but her words were powerful and meaningful. Though it was a bit of a surprise, I understood what she was on about. I believed in her and I shrugged it off as we laughed in unison. It was a day of sharing as we sat on the lawns enjoying a barbecue lunch provided for the celebration of National Aboriginal Day. The day was beautiful and pleasant and sunny.

Meeting with a friend who suffers from depression, we go shopping or sit at her house and share our experiences chatting about our illnesses. We both suffer with bipolar. My friend would sit quietly in deep thought as she normally does. I would be the opposite, talking erratically, stirring her. 'Wake up,' I would say loudly, the atmosphere moving with excitement as her visitors arrived. I sit motionless with amazement. I should be home, I say to myself.

Hell, I get tired; my expectations become overwhelmed. I need to take time out to meditate in my own space. I do this by just stepping out my back door to hear the birds, the silence and to enjoy the simplicity. I don't have money to spend on myself but I do take care of my own well-being. My time and space and enjoyment are at home. I enjoy taking time out in my garden and playing harmonica in the presence of my grandchildren.

The need for help

There is help and assistance and awareness and understanding in the community today about mental health, and organisations that can assist you with your well-being. However, there are a lot of people who still need help and who are not receiving it. The government have closed down many wards. It is quite difficult to enter into a psychiatric ward even when you are unwell. You have to be suffering with a severe bout of manic depression. The government should consider the rights of those who desperately need help, not just sweep the subject under the carpet. I have sat and spoken to many people who suffer mental health. We need to be heard. There are not enough facilities for the mentally ill.

Shame

Many of my friends and people do not fully understand mental illness. Well, here's this wonderful word again! SPIRITUAL BREAKDOWN. I hate the word 'mental'; it's a stigma for all of us who suffer this illness.

I have experienced shame because of my illness, in the fact that I have been hospitalised. If people who make me feel this were in my body, then they would understand. Being disorientated with memory loss can generate shame too, when all of a sudden you would have to be reminded of an incident and you have no memory but just have to go along with the story.

Friends

My contacts with friends and family keeps me alert. Mina is a humble young mother who has suffered an injury that left her brain in trauma. I have spent some time with Mina. We have often sat and spoken and shared our experiences and laughed together and also cried. She would say, 'You know, Aunty Doris, we need to release it and cleanse our body with tears, with comfort and sharing our illnesses.' For me, it's not only healing for her but also for me to talk it out and to have that connection with the realities of friends that suffer depression, grief or sadness. It is a good feeling to be able to come away smiling.

Sharing with my people

One of my earliest experiences was to visit the Flinders Ranges *Iga Warta* to share with the Adnyamathanha culture. We camped on the site from 11 to 15 October 2002. We were welcomed by the leader. This was a journey of healing as we met the elders with deepest respect and joined as one in celebration with guidance of the staff.

It all began with the Link Up organisation of Nunkuwarrin Yunti. A group of the Stolen Generations went on a journey to *Iga Warta*. Our visit was to the sacred site, the cave paintings. A large group of us walked the long trail to the cave. It was a very moving and emotional time for all of us. We trod the rocky dry creek on what seemed to be a long journey. This place was a beginning for healing all of us we walked with solace as we neared the caves with the guide.

The Adnyamathanha people played host to us and shared their stories we sat with the woman to do paintings. I did a painting with assistance from an Adnyamathanha woman as she told me her story. I asked questions on the design I was doing, she was helpful and guided me. I moved on to something more challenging in making a boomerang and claps stick.

During this stay, we learnt to share the culture of the Flinders Ranges people with greatest respect, something we could bring back to our homes and to share from a culture that is strong. It taught me to respect other Aboriginal cultures and it was a time to heal the pain, and to connect with the spiritual aspect in this wonderful country of many cultures in our communities.

Walk with respect

We walk the trail with respect
We learn the culture
The land is ours to share
Our spirits are not broken
We walk together with laughter
To connect with accepting a culture so strong
A time to our broken spirit

Kumerangk

At about the same time, we gathered for celebration of the first viewing of *Kumerangk* around the nation. The women gathered at Sandra's house to have a joyous night. It was a night to celebrate as we watched the making of *Kumerangk* on SBS. The group of woman had strength and motivation. A few tears were shed and laughter could be heard. It was good to see the elders and my older sister Doreen weep with happiness. This certainly was a time to share. It opened up my heart to understand my heritage.

Hospitalisation

The times that I have spent in hospital are times that one will never forget. One cannot erase these memories – to me, it is a spiritual breakdown. The process of being admitted into hospital can be invasive, making us feel uneasy. It can make you laugh and it can make you cry, so laugh with me and join my 'wonderful journeys'.

The wards constantly vibrate with movements of patients, some of whom can become quite vocal. As for privacy, often there's none. A ward could be bursting with excitement and also with sadness in patients that I had become friends with.

In the hospital, some of the patients can adjust and are able take part in activities. But this is difficult for some who may be heavily sedated. In some centres, patients are wandering around smoking quite heavily in a closed courtyard, some quite restless at times, some sitting in a quiet motionless position, some who may be boisterous, minds racing with confusion. I had seen all this. There were times that I was in control and times that I would be uncontrollable.

Once when I had taken an overdose to end my life, I spent a short time in hospital. I was woken suddenly with a nurse covering me quickly as I lay cross the bed peaceably until the doctor came to see me. I was shamed by the nurse's action, as my 'mania' was exposed in to the whole bloody ward in an undignified manner. God knows how long I was uncovered. I was not in the position to cover myself. As I think back, I know that I could have spent more time with the doctor. He had little time for me as I was still coming through the overdose. He leant over me asking me questions. How in the hell am I supposed to answer him in my state of mind? Before I knew it, I was then taken to Woodleigh House to a psychiatric ward.

The memory of one of my stays in this *wurengi* institution, Glenside Hospital, I will never forget. As I was really unwell at this time and finding it difficult to queue in line just like at Colebrook (the home I was raised in after being removed from my family), it was like reliving patterns of the past. Waiting and shuffling our feet in a line to be served our meals, not a pretty sight. It was a difficult task for me to eat my food, choking on it, vomiting, feeling quite ill. I obviously became unmanageable and was put in a padded room. The time in the padded rooms, although I am vague about it, was a very threatening experience. The fear of isolation was intense and phobic. It seemed my heart was pounding in rhythm to the noise I could still hear outside.

I do believe that there is a breakdown in hospitals when one is suicidal or has attempted suicide. You are in the dark about what is happening to you. Lack of communication with hospital staff causes bewilderment and doesn't help you in adjusting to the ordeal you have just been through. I have never been successful in communicating with a psychiatrist. It never made sense to me. Jargon only complicated my feelings about survival.

Not enough is done in this situation. No follow-up with referrals, and I was left with confusion and in isolation, with no direction or further help. Attempts should be made to follow up those of indigenous background who suffer with mental illness. The support when one is to go home from the hospital is crucial. I have experienced the isolation, with feelings of not being heard and not having contact with a single soul. I have survived throughout my bouts of illness, but there can be danger ahead with suicidal thoughts for those who have been through what I have experienced.

Hospital again

I admitted myself to Woodleigh House as my thoughts were racing, with issues that were out of control. I took the bare essentials. I had rung ACIC on numerous occasions. Then, following advice, at two-thirty a.m. I drove myself to hospital. Feeling strong and confident, with bloodshot eyes, I headed to this place, hoping to rest my head, a place with understanding staff.

I interacted with younger patients the next day. I was flitting from the main ward to the psych ward, flying like a bird with racing thoughts. However, somehow I found a quiet time to paint a pine cone in preparation for the Christmas season.

I received bad news about one of my sisters from Colebrook Home. She had died five years ago in Brisbane. I never knew she had passed away until that moment. I took the grieving in my stride but was saddened with the news.

I am feeling that I am not alone with this illness. I am strong. I am free and have freedom of choice. Hey! I am not a failure. I have had the ability to write my memoirs. It's time to rest my body and soul after an early bath; it's time to shut eyes wide open.

I look for a cigarette, thinking only of my family. I look for a lighter and find not only one but two – a bonus.

The time was eleven-thirty p.m. and I rose from my bed in the ward. Feeling restless, I spoke to the nurses who were on duty. I thought I had done something wrong. The nurse convinced me that I was all right and not to worry. I asked for a cigarette. I wandered from my bedroom, down the corridor to the nurses' bay, reciting the Lord's Prayer. I was tearful and emotional and asked for a cigarette again and

I was allowed to go downstairs. I was in control of my emotions as I entered the smoke room, an area that is opened to the skies.

I had stood only a few minutes when Adam, a young man who I had met and befriended previously, walked in to join me. We at this moment stood religiously. It was ironic and overwhelming. I spontaneously thought of Adam and Eve. We talked to the nurses. 'He's got the whole world in his hands.' I thought of the first chapter in the Bible – God created heaven and earth then man and woman Adam and Eve.

Religion comes to me on many occasions when I am unwell. I often pose as Jesus on the crucifix, as I did once on a pool table at Glenside, much to the dislike of two other patients who were playing at the time. Mulpurini Doris Kartinyeri is Eve! This is how I feel when I am unwell.

Trauma

I have been on this long journey of years of trauma to get to where I am now: the trauma of being stolen as a babe in arms and placed in an institution for fourteen years, losing my family, identity and culture.

The trauma of connecting with my family had a profound effect on me in later years. I believe this was the beginning and cause of my illness through the years of adjusting to so many new surroundings through my teens and womanhood. The Stolen Generations era had a horrendous and astounding effect on me.

Decisions

With the highs and lows, there are times that I need to pursue to my own personal need of making a decision.

In April 1994 I made an important decision: I chose to write about my life, to complete my books as a capable individual.

I have accepted the fact that I will sometimes live in confusion and that I am guided by my own decision. I am a gifted individual with personal needs of being in contact with my family. I force myself to write to tell my story of my difficulties as a sufferer of bipolar.

All my life I have struggled to survive with the loss of my families, the loss of my culture, my language and the loss of myself. But I rebuilt my life. I left one institution, then another: a mental institution. And I raised a family and ran a home. I have survived, I am a survivor.

The day begins

With anticipation, I lie in bed with racing thoughts about what plans I have for today. The early news on my bedside clock radio brings me nothing but negativity. I live in two worlds in which I must survive: a world of poverty and the world of the rich. My richness is from the heart. The scare tactics are out there.

It's August, the cold morning is crisp as I write at odd hours. I am in control as I write. I take heed and listen to my words in the stillness of the morning. I hear a car squeal as I write. I hear the clock ticking, but not to my pace. My heart beats in silence as I sip a glass of cold milk. 'Listen to the rhythm of the falling rain' – a song enters my mind from the past.

My past is what is present today. Sometimes it is hard to tell the difference. The dictators are at it again with scare tactics. We are manipulated with awful news. This awfullising keeps us where we are.

I fill my mind with positive thoughts to begin this brand-new day. The well-being of myself and my family is important to me. I sat in the car the other day with my youngest daughter April. A song came on air by Laurie London – 'He's got the hold world in his hands'. Well, did we sing and clap with harmony and with much joy!

My family are fine, my grandchildren are fine with the nurturing all around and, with me being a role model, things can look up. The concerns are there as I struggle to look beyond what seems. We all have issues. I don't need dictators telling me how many smokes I can have, or where to smoke them. I have my smokes. In my comfort zone, I do what is best for me. My determination gives me confidence and I have assurance from others, from friends and family. But I am in control. I am making my own decisions right now.

The future

I have grieved for many of my people who have passed away in the last few months. I have grieved for my mother. She has long gone and life must go on and I must live for the present, and I now grieve for my sister Doreen. I must move on but my life and past has often been horrific for me. I have had a lot of support from Link Up. I am so grateful for them. I feel that God can only heal if you have Christian beliefs. I do have Christian beliefs and hope one day I can heal.

So here I am many years on and managing my medications, having my ups and downs, highs and lows. But most times I consider myself normal. If my writings appear all over the place, well, they are! It is difficult to recollect where my mind has been as I go from one mind to another. This is me, this is who I am.

As I sit in the early morning sunshine with my daughter and my grandson doing art and craft and using modelling clay, I can make whatever I want with it. Just like my life. I will embrace the present when I am well and manage the best I can when I am not. I will look forward to the laughs with family and friends when I recall my events.

I don't want my life to be obscured with complications. It's time for me to focus on me and to do what I enjoy without complicating things. The world is crowded with stress and anxiety. The greatest issue that I cannot comprehend is that mental health is an illness about which many people are still ignorant.

I consider myself to be an outgoing individual and I live to write, which I enjoy. I live with confusions but I live to tell my stories as a sufferer of bipolar. My space is mine and there are struggles that at times I have to endure and I have learnt to take control of these.

My struggles have been rewarded by my achievements in writing.

The biggest reward was the launch of my autobiography, *Kick the Tin*. Since that, I've also published my children's book, *Bush Games and Knuckle Bones*.

I fight with determination to survive my illness. The determination of my survival has given me strength to continue with my writing, even though I have scars in the past. The turmoil and the tears have been the part of experiences of learning and of healing.

I always reflect to the past and to my culture when I become ill. The true spiritual nature of my Aboriginality plays an important part in my life. I have a strong belief in the Aboriginal culture and my people. I want to be part of them, to dance with their spirits and share my strong needs to be part of them.

My name is Mulparinni Doris Kartinyeri. I am a strong woman who believes that my culture, my heritage and my beliefs were taken from me. I have to learn to laugh as I write and I smile as I read my manuscript. It has been hard for me to write this book, but I have a better understanding of my illness. I have connected with my well-being.

The good news is that I have done it, with the help of my writing. I have developed strength, I have learned to have control, moving on with the help of friends and the support of Woodleigh House, a psych ward of supportive staff.

My memories of my past are still vivid. I wake early at the crack of dawn. The birds are swooning with excitement at this time of the day. Sunrise is beyond the hills. The sounds of the birds assure me of the beauty of this planet and through the many years of bipolar my passion for trees and plants has provided much joy for me. I have nurtured them as they have nurtured me.

It is important to me for us as people to connect to the land as a strong and thriving nation, recognising our own identity. As an individual and an Indigenous woman from Australia, I am learning from the many cultures. This vast country Australia generates energy and for me that is spiritual, In the morning I wake to hear the birds singing in the trees, playing in the background every day, bringing me much pleasure and being very affirming to me.

Most important to me is that I have found my family. I will be positive. I will be strong and continue to be strong in my writing. I must do this for my family.

www.ingramcontent.com/pod-product-compliance
Lightning Source LLC
Chambersburg PA
CBHW030912080526
44589CB00010B/267